POCKET IMAGES

Edlington,
Maltby &
Warmsworth

Yorkshire Main colliery, Edlington.

Cover illustration: The author playing an elf in a Christmas play at Warmsworth Low Road West infants' school, December 1958.

POCKET IMAGES

Edlington, Maltby & Warmsworth

Peter Tuffrey

NONSUCH

Building Warmsworth roundabout.

First published 2000
This new pocket edition 2007
Images unchanged from first edition

Nonsuch Publishing Limited
Cirencester Road, Chalford,
Stroud, Gloucestershire, GL6 8PE
www.nonsuch-publishing.com

Nonsuch Publishing is an imprint of NPI Media Group

© Peter Tuffrey, 2000

The right of Peter Tuffrey to be identified as the Author
of this work has been asserted in accordance with the
Copyrights, Designs and Patents Act 1988.

British Library Cataloguing in Publication Data.
A catalogue record for this book is available from the British Library.

ISBN 978-1-84588-401-7

Typesetting and origination by Nonsuch Publishing Limited
Printed in Great Britain by Oaklands Book Services Limited

Contents

Acknowledgements

I would like to thank the following people for their help: Doug Brown, Tommy Emms, Jim Firth, Margaret Glarvey, Geoff Hawker, Nigel Kaye, Jimmy Kelly, Brian Lowe, Jane Medley, Brenda Mitchell, Hugh Parkin, Robert Sanderson, Andrew Tasker, T. Walters, Gerry Wakelin, Tony Wormley.

This book is dedicated to the memory of Derek Cartwright

The White House at Warmsworth, now demolished.

Introduction

Compiling this book has been particularly satisfying for me, knowing all three areas very well. I lived in Warmsworth between 1954 and 1979, and returned to reside there in 1996. I attended Edlington comprehensive school from 1966 to 1970, and have regularly journeyed through Maltby while travelling to and from Sheffield. Also, in my younger days, I regularly played football for Warmsworth primary school and Edlington comprehensive, and we often met teams from Maltby.

Some people may question why I have linked the three areas together in a book, especially when Edlington and Warmsworth are in the Doncaster area, and Maltby is in the Rotherham area. To begin with, all three follow each other on a winding route extending south-west from Doncaster. The mining developments during the early part of the twentieth century at Edlington and Maltby closely mirrored each other. Also, many pupils at Warmsworth and Edlington, who, over the years, passed their eleven-plus, attended Maltby Grammar School. Thus I feel that, in some ways, the three areas are inextricably linked.

In the Edlington section, we have a small glimpse at the rural atmosphere in the area, prior to the sinking of the Yorkshire Main colliery. One of these photographs, featured at the top of p.12, is beautifully composed by James Simmonton & Sons, whose work has been featured on a number of occasions in this series of publications. While there are no pictures included of the sod-cutting ceremony at Yorkshire Main, or indeed of the sinkers, there are, nevertheless, some interesting views dating from the colliery's early years of operation. Those taken during the 1920s showing the colliery deputies reveal some fascinating historical details. Perhaps the photographs I like best in this section are those featuring the funeral of colliery fireman Tommy Hayes. A coffin being carried on a fire engine is quite a unique, if not a surreal, sight.

I thought I was quite fortunate to obtain some pictures of Edlington Victoria Road School during the 1950s. For these, I am indebted to the co-operation of the headmistress, Janice Middleton, who was the only one out of the ten heads of schools that I contacted in the area who responded to my request for information or pictures. None of the others were forthcoming—a sad sign of the times?

The most dramatic Edlington pictures are those showing the conflict between pickets and police during the 1984/85 miners' strike. In the final pages of the Edlington section, several colliery buildings are seen being felled and the site redeveloped, adding a final chapter to the pit's history.

The Maltby section, similar to the Edlington one, shows the area first in its rural splendour and then through its development into a thriving mining community.

Several pictures also illustrate scenes at the time of the two disasters, which occurred during the early years of the colliery's operation. Later, we have a glimpse of life underground, and for these views I am indebted to the colliery staff for making them available. The pit still thrives today and, later in the section, there are some pictures depicting major reconstruction work taking place on the site.

The sinking of Yorkshire Main had only a small effect on the rural outlook of Warmsworth, albeit only a mile a way from the hive of mining activity. Houses were built on Edlington Lane, and Wrightson and Cecil Avenues were established to house miners. The Balby tram route was extended from Oswin Avenue to Warmsworth as a feeder service to the colliery. Furthermore, the Barrell Inn licence was transferred from the heart of the sleepy village to more commodious premises at the Sheffield Road crossroads. In spite of all this, Warmsworth retained its rural charm until the post-War years when a number of fields were developed for both public and private housing. The most dramatic development in Warmsworth's history occurred in the early 1960s, when a by-pass was extended through the village's eastern periphery. High Road was widened and since this time the area has become a most desirable dormitory village; residents finding easy access from there to all points of the country.

Personally, I find it a little unnerving to be on photographs included in what is essentially an old photograph book. But some are over forty years old, and no doubt they will be of great interest to many people now, and in years to come.

View along Sheffield Road at Warmsworth, with the Cecil Hotel in the distance on the right.

One

Edlington

The Greyhound's Monument in Edlington Wood. The *Doncaster Chronicle* of 1 May 1914 gave some details about this curious monument: '[A]mongst the trees, and just beside [a] cottage there stands a monument to a dog, placed there by its graceful master, Robert Molesworth, in 1714. Small boys playing about will assert that the dog killed a lion. Others state that it is Gelert's tomb. But Gelert is in no way connected with the dog whose memorial is in Edlington Wood. Of this dog it is related that once it saved its master's life. Details have been handed down of this incident. The master wished to enter a certain room, but was prevented by the dog who gripped his coat. Again he moved towards the room, and again, the dog intervened. Curious to know the meaning of this strange behaviour he told a servant to go into the room. The latter obeyed, but, on opening the door, was immediately shot dead by an armed burglar, who had concealed himself there, intending to remain in hiding until the family had retired for the night. The monument consists of an urn placed upon a square pedestal; the whole stands about seven feet high, and is surrounded by wooden palings. On one side of the pedestal is carved in relief a greyhound ...'

The Greyhound's Monument, in
Edlington Wood.

In the Year 1714. Robert Molesworth
Esqr (afterwards Viscount Molesworth) sent to
London the remains of his favourite do[g]
and buried them in Edlington Wood.
The following lines are a translation
of the Latin inscription on the monument.

Stay traveller,
Nor wonder that a lamented dog.
Is thus interred with funeral honours.
But ah! what a dog!
His beautiful form and snow white co[at]
Pleasing manners and sporting play[ful]
Affection, obedience, & fidelity
Made him the delight of his master
To whose side he closely adhered.
With his eager companions of the ch[ase]
Delighted in attending him.
Whenever the mind of his lord was depre[ssed]
He would assume fresh spirit and animat[ion]
A master not ungrateful for his service[s]
Has here in tears, deposited his remain[s]
In this marble urn.

M.F.C.
i.e.
Molesworth fieri curavit. 171[4]

J. Simonton & Sons,
Photographers. Balby. Doncaster

Another view of the Greyhound's Monument. Part of the inscription on the postcard view, taken by J. Simonton & Sons of Balby, reads: 'In the year 1714, Robert Molesworth Esq. (afterwards Viscount Molesworth) sent from London the remains of his favourite dog and buried them in Edlington Wood.'

View of the pump and house in Edlington Wood. Lady Isabella Battie-Wrightson of Cusworth Park was formerly lady of the manor and owned all the land with the exception of Edlington Wood; the property of Edlington was purchased by the lord of the manor in 1803 from the co-heiress of the Molesworth family, who formerly had a manor house here, near the church.

Kelly's *West Riding* directory (1908) notes that Edlington Wood, the property of Earl Fitzwilliam DSO, contains about 400 acres, divided into ridings by roads converging to a centre, where stands the 'Woodman's House'. Within the wood are the remains of an entrenchment, called 'Double Dykes'. Edlington's population in 1901 was 158.

Edlington Wood House. The *Doncaster Chronicle* of 1 May 1914 said that a popular resort of the inhabitants of Doncaster was Edlington Wood, about two miles south-west of the Balby tram terminus at Oswin Avenue. 'Intersected as it is by grass-grown paths, several pleasant strolls may be taken in the wood, which is charming in the spring and early summer. Light refreshments can be obtained at a cottage amongst the trees.'

Rural scene at Edlington. On 13 March 1911 the *Doncaster Gazette* gave some indication of the transformation that would soon overcome Edlington in the following piece: 'Doncaster people are by this time fairly familiar with the rapid transformations of the countryside which follow on the colliery developments in any particular part of their neighbourhood. Such a metamorphosis is going on apace at the present time between Warmsworth and Edlington, in the neighbourhood of the new Yorkshire Main colliery, where acres of quiet agricultural land are being converted into a modern colliery village, the home of the teeming population that will flock into the district within the next few months when the Barnsley Bed is reached.'

A group posing on land which was soon to be laid out for housing. Victoria Road, Shaw Road, Queen's Crescent and King's Crescent are among the streets built on the area. Yorkshire Main Colliery and the York Hotel can be seen in the background. The hotel was built in 1913.

Above and below: Yorkshire Main colliery was situated in the parish of Edlington. The *Transactions of the Doncaster & District Mining Society* for August 1937 mentions that two shafts, each 21ft 6in finished diameter but widened out in the middle, were sunk to the Barnsley Bed, which was reached at a depth of 907 yards. The thickness of the seam, the only one worked, was 5ft 6in to 6ft with bag coal roof and clunch floor. It was wound from a greater depth than any other colliery in Yorkshire. The sinking was commenced in December 1909 and completed in July 1911. The No. 1 shaft, brick-lined throughout, was widened out at 399 yards until at 405 yards it attained a diameter of 24ft 6in. The No. 2 shaft, also brick-lined throughout, was widened out in a similar manner to No. 1.

Above and below: Deputies posing with lamps and sticks at Yorkshire Main. Identified in the above picture are Bill Richards, George Wanless, George Watson, Tommy Edwards and Steve Bunting. Note that one of the deputies on the front row has a detonator bag. In both pictures, the men are posing near the fan house. In the early days, it was understood that the Edlington colliers were mostly drawn from Derbyshire and Nottinghamshire. The original method of working at Yorkshire Main was by longwall faces, divided into 'tub stalls', the coal being hand-filled into tubs on the coal face. In 1933, the 'tub stalls' system was replaced by the method of longwall advancing coal faces with conveyors along the coal face and a central roadway conveyor to transport the coal to a loading point on the main roadway in settled ground behind the working face.

Above and below: Members of Edlington's Yorkshire Main Cricket Club are depicted in these two pictures. Amongst those seen in the bottom picture are: Freddie Hutchinson, Johnny Pear and Fred Hanford. Colliery teams once formed the backbone of the Doncaster & District Cricket League, formed in 1912. In 1926, out of a total playing strength of forty-six, twenty-four were sponsored by collieries. Also, there was also always a generous sprinkling of miners on the playing strength of the village clubs. The Edlington club won the Second Division Championship in 1932.

Left and below: Two workplace scenes at Yorkshire Main. The colliery was situated on land belonging to Lady Isabella Battie-Wrightson, of Cusworth Hall, and owned by the Staveley Coal & Iron Co. Ltd, Chesterfield, of which Henry Westlake was Managing Director, and C.P. Markham Chairman of Directors. The agent was R.W. Cuthbertson of Staveley; the manager J. Neal; under-manager Robert Clayton; engineer, B.J. Marson; engine-wright, S. Clarke; electrical engineer, W. Chappel.

Opposite above: Edlington Victoria Road school. On 27 June 1913 the *Doncaster Chronicle* stated: 'Edlington boasts some of the finest elementary schools in the country, which are just now approaching completion. The schools are situated on Princess Crescent [at the junction with Victoria Road], and are near the colliery. They are right in the centre of the new village. They have not been erected for an excess population, but for the population that will flow into—that is flowing into—the village. They are the largest and finest schools in the district, and are built on the quadrangle principle; that is, the school buildings are ranged on four sides of a square, in the centre of which is a lawn, as is the case at Maltby. But the building at Edlington will accommodate more children than the one at Maltby, and will have one more class-room than at that place. The cost too, is greater, totalling as it does to over £11,000.'

A picnic gathering in Edlington Woods, c.1905. The group of people is thought to include a Mrs Robinson and a Mrs Stevenson.

Above and below: Scenes at Yorkshire Main colliery, Edlington. The *Doncaster Gazette* of 21 July 1911 said that the erection of the engine house, the supply of surface plant and the construction of the head gear were all well in hand before a sod of ground was turned for the sinking. This part of the operation was commenced on 13 December 1909.

YORKSHIRE MAIN NO I

Above: Members of Edlington Local Labour Party's women's section, which is thought to include the names of Peat, Tucker, Tait, Eckles, McNicholas, and Bickwell.

Below: Scene at Yorkshire Main Colliery, Edlington. It was stated that in the early stages of the work on the colliery, the sinkers were somewhat hampered by that *bête noire* of colliery engineers in South Yorkshire—the influx of water from the limestone strata. Fortunately, however, the difficulty was not nearly so serious as at Bulcroft, where the services of German freezing experts had to be engaged, but it required the constant use of powerful pumps to keep the inrushing water 'baled out' while the shafts were being carried down beyond the affected region. The progress of the work was comparatively free from serious accidents, though one sinker lost his life in April 1910.

The *Doncaster Chronicle* of 20 June 1913 announced: 'Edlington now enjoys the dignity of its own station [opened in 1912]. It is only a "halt", it is true, but it is conveniently situated on the fringe of the village, and provides a railway link with Wakefield and a number of intervening colliery centres, which means of locomotion is found very useful indeed. The little station is on the Dearne Valley Railway new line, on the road between Warmsworth and Edlington, and there is a daily service of four trains between Edlington and Wakefield, but no Sunday service.'

DEARNE VALLEY RAILWAY
RAIL MOTOR CAR TICKET.
Issued subject to the regulations and conditions in the
Company's Time Tables, Books, Bills and Notices.
Must be shewn on demand.
Passengers should not accept tickets unless passed through
the Bell Punch in their presence.

HARLINGTON to
EDLINGTON FOR BALBY (Doncaster) or
Edlington for Balby (Doncaster) to HARLINGTON

B

Fare 4½d

A Dearne Valley Railway motor car ticket.

Edlington Lane with the York Hotel in the distance on the right. Although the Yorkshire Main colliery was owned by the Staveley Coal & Iron Company, which also had the paramount interest in the Brodsworth undertaking, there was no intention to repeat the Woodlands model village experiment, under the direct auspices of the colliery owners, at Edlington. On the other hand, the housing of the miners who would work at the Edlington colliery was not to be left to the haphazard efforts of the speculative builder. Something between the two was the principle upon which the Edlington colliery village was to be developed—it was laid out on a single, comprehensive plan, approved by the colliery company, but the actual building was left to private enterprise.

During June 1913 a reporter from the *Doncaster Chronicle* visited Edlington and wrote the following: 'Streets of substantially built houses, everyone of them occupied, and with plenty of space and light and ventilation between the thoroughfares, come into view on the right as one enters the new village by deviation from the Warmsworth Road, and to the left is the colliery. As a background we have the green and glorious Woods. Houses appear to be at a premium, and building is still rapidly proceeding. The mortar machines were merrily mixing on the occasion of our visit, and the tinkle of the trowel came from all directions.'

St John's church, Edlington. The *Doncaster Chronicle* of 16 January 1914 reported: 'We are able today to make the interesting announcement that the handsome new church which is being erected at Edlington new village to serve the mining community there is fast approaching completion and that it will be dedicated on February 2nd ... The new church, which is one of those under the South Yorks Coalfields Church Extension Scheme follows much the same lines as that at Maltby, being in the Lombardy or Romanesque style of architecture. It occupies a commanding position at the head of the main avenue of the village, the site having been generously given by the Edlington Land and Development Syndicate. Accommodation is provided for about 500 worshippers. The building has a campanile, this being designed in keeping with the Romanesque character ...'

Scene at the stone-laying ceremony, St John's church, Edlington. During June 1913, the Revd E. Odling, the curate in charge at Edlington, told the *Doncaster Chronicle* of his excitement of the laying of the foundation stone of the new St John's church at Edlington. This was to take place on St John the Baptist's Day, 24 June, the ceremony being performed by Mrs Warde-Aldam, and the religious service being conducted by the Bishop of Sheffield.

Right and below: Edlington's peace celebrations on 19 July 1919, where it was stated that the whole village turned out. And, from the first bang on the drum, when the procession commenced its tour in the morning, to the last dying embers of the enormous bonfire which ended the festivities, there was a ceaseless round of rejoicing. The procession followed the following route: Edlington Lane, Low Warmsworth, Sheffield Road, Cecil Avenue, Edlington Lane, returning to New Village, Edlington. During the procession, the judges examined the decorated houses.

PEACE DAY CELEBRATIONS AT EDLINGTON JULY 19-1919

Above and below: Around 9 p.m., when the distribution of prizes had finished, all eyes instinctively turned towards the hill on which stood Edlington's link in the chain of beacons. Everybody was impatient for the fireworks. It was laid down by the authorities that all the beacons in the chain should be lit at 11 p.m. However, Edlington villagers decided to light theirs a little earlier so that it might be burning merrily at 11 p.m.

Right and below: The funeral took place on Thursday 15 January 1931 of Thomas Hayes, aged fifty-eight, of 25 Carr Road, Edlington, who had died after a short illness. Tommy Hayes was an underground official at Yorkshire Main and for the previous eight years had been chief of the colliery fire brigade. Before going to Edlington he was a member of the Brodsworth Colliery fire brigade, where he received the ten years' service medal. The Yorkshire Main colliery brigade had received several calls during the period Tommy Hayes had held office and had many times been congratulated on their promptness and smartness.

Tommy was an enthusiastic gardener and beekeeper, and because of his genial and generous disposition was very popular, not only in Edlington, but for miles around Doncaster. The coffin was carried on one of the Doncaster County Borough Brigade fire engines. Thirty-five firemen attended the funeral, including members of the Yorkshire Main, Doncaster borough, Brodsworth colliery, Conisbrough, Mexborough and South Elmsall brigades, and also the Edlington Ambulance Brigade.

Scene at Yorkshire Main with the colliery ambulance. Tommy Hawker is on the left and Albert Church on the right. The fan house is in the distance on the right.

Edlington Victoria Road school, c.1926. Those identified include Geoff Hawker, Stan Glover, 'Lank' Hainsworth, Eddy Hardy, Fred Brown, Billy Wheat, Frank Cope, Harold Parkes, William Whetton.

Opposite below: Yorkshire Main fire brigade posing in the pit yard. Amongst those identified are Jos Gawthorpe (under-manager), Lawrie Beardsley, Johnny Walker (manager). The buildings in the background include the engine house, blacksmith's shop and boiler house.

Edlington Victoria Road school, c.1932. From left to right, back row: -?-, Bill Parkin, -?-, Henry Littleford, Ivor Challis, Jack Selkirk, Bill Whetton, -?-, -?-. Second row: Cope, Joe Hanford, -?-, Joe Orton, -?-, Jeff Hancock, Cec Dungworth, Arthur Davis. Third row: John Dowd, -?-, Dennis Tatham, Cyril Faulkner. Fourth row: -?-, John Edwards, Bill Wheat, Ken Riley, Tom Mould, Harold Siddall, Albert Lawson. Front row: -?-, Norman Evans, Charlie Tate, Geoff Hawker, Howard Crane, Charlie Street, -?-, Stan Glover.

Scene along Duke's Crescent, Edlington. The new village was built under the control of the Edlington Land & Development Company, of which Harry Davies of Cardiff was the chairman of directors. They had bought from the Colliery Company about 50 acres of land in the vicinity of the pit and the site was laid out by Messrs T.E. Richards and Haye, of Cardiff, Pontypridd and Doncaster. The land was bought in plots or taken on lease by private builders, but they had to conform to the plan and the regulations laid down as to the construction and types of the houses.

Edlington Victoria Road school football team, winners of the Gundry Shield in 1934. From left to right, back row: Geoff Hawker, Jack Selkirk, Jim Morrer, 'Tiny' Adlington. Middle row: Bill Whetton, Arthur Davies, Jackie Shaw, Charlie Jones, Ted Clarke. Front row: George Brewster, Bob Barrass. Jackie Shaw eventually played for Rotherham United and Sheffield Wednesday. The shield was in memory of William Richard Gundry, a noted and respected character from the previous century. Gundry was a teacher and then headmaster at King Edward Road school, Balby, between 1908 and 1922, when he died aged sixty-one. He was also the founder and chairman of Doncaster and District Schools Football Association. His obituary paid a glowing tribute to his talents and skills and displayed the respect and admiration felt by others: 'Esteemed by his staff, respected by his boys, affectionately regarded by the whole community, Mr Gundry leaves vacant a big place in the life of Balby. His death is a loss not only to his own family circle, but to Balby and the town as a whole.'

Left: Construction work at Yorkshire Main Colliery.

Below: Scene in Yorkshire Main Colliery yard where a boiler has been transported by the vehicle depicted.

Grocer and confectioner Randolf Churchill Hopkinson started in business around 1913 in a very small way in Stanhope Road, Wheatley, Doncaster. By 1925, besides his headquarters in Copley Road, he had no fewer that eight branch shops. Hopkinson was one of those quick to realize that the mining community at Edlington would one day become very large and, shortly after he started in Stanhope Road, he used to send out groceries in a hand barrow to the pit village. Soon his custom there grew to such an extent that he purchased a horse and dray. That was perhaps the beginning of the large delivery business he built up during the ensuing years. At one time he had seven motor vehicles delivering provisions over an area of 15 miles around Doncaster. About 1915, Hopkinson opened his first branch in Edlington (pictured here) and it was said that the venture proved to be thoroughly justified. R.C. Hopkinson retired around 1948 and died aged sixty-six in 1954.

Above and below: Around 1920, Harold Sanderson, a native of Holmfirth, and son of a weaver, purchased a lock-up butcher's shop in Edlington from a Mr Lodge. Previously, Harold had worked for Quarmby's in Holmfirth. He did not live in Edlington but in nearby Warmsworth and eventually established a thriving family butcher's business. He also supplied meat to schools in the area. He did not kill beasts on the premises but took them to the Doncaster Corporation slaughterhouse. In an average week, Harold would sell meat from three bullocks, three pigs and eight sheep. Other butchers in Edlington included Hather's, Poynter's, Glasbey's and the Co-operative. In 1949 Harold's son Robert, aged twenty-seven, joined him in the business. Robert

had been trained with Farm Stores in French Gate. Shortly after Robert joined the business, the premises were refurbished by the Sheffield firm of Barlow's. On land let from a farmer in Warmsworth, Robert kept lambs and up to 1,000 hens. Harold retired in the late 1950s, and died in 1968. He had never involved himself in public life. Robert closed the business, c.1962.

Above: Members of the Edlington and Warmsworth C District fire service, pictured in around 1940 at the AFS fire station at the rear of the Royal Hotel, Edlington. The picture includes Joe Beckett, Jack Everton, Arthur Heaton, Frank Lawrence, Arthur Harris and Robert Sanderson.

Below: A formal group in Yorkshire Main yard, *c*.1950. From left to right, back row: Freddie Hutchinson, Freddie Davison, Tommy Oliver, Danny Gay, Cyril Cooke, Tommy Lawrence, ? Edwards, Albert Baracliffe, Andy Cusac, Hughie Lewis, Lewis, Percy York, Ernest Frost. Middle row: Chris Thornycroft, Harry Unwin, Arthur Wood, Wilf Wallis, Bill Hilton, Reuben Spiers, Bill Carter, Albert Church, Arthur Holes, George Wanless, Horace Gater, Ned Reed, Bill Templeton, Tom Emms. Front row: Bill Lounds, George Bailey, Albert Rose, Albert Julians, Jack Edwards, Len Bates, Bob Grainger, Fred Beevers, Edgar Howe, Turner Ball, George Watson.

St Peter's church, Edlington. Magilton (1977) includes the following in his comments about the structure: 'Small, two-cell Norman with north aisle heavily buttressed addition, and tower at west end. South porch contains re-used north mouldings ... Chancel arch also Norman, as is corbel table (very rare) ... Massive buttresses support tower at west end ... The Norman church, although small, is an indicator of substantial early medieval settlement in the area, a guess confirmed by Domesday ... The relatively unaltered state of the church might be taken to imply a lack of prosperity in the later medieval period.'

The *Doncaster Gazette* of 6 May 1965 carried an article about Edlington church under the headline 'Future of Old Church in the Balance', and gave the following information: 'Since the last restoration work ten years ago [the church] has been disused and in the intervening years vandals have damaged parts of the building including the roof, chancel and windows.' Mr John Orr, secretary of the Sheffield Diocesan Board of Finance, said there was no longer support for the church and there seemed to be no parishioners. He thought possibly former parishioners had moved away or died. People in the area now attended St Peter's, Warmsworth, or St John's, Edlington. The picture here shows the chancel at St Peter's church, Edlington.

Right: A classroom view at Victoria Road school, Edlington, during the mid-1950s. H.R. Wormald in *Modern Doncaster* (1973) noted: 'The Education Act, 1944, had placed public education of all types in the hands of County Councils and County Boroughs. The school leaving age was raised to fifteen years and a new pattern of education, namely primary and secondary, became the guiding lines for the local authorities ... Over the years the major projects were the implementation of the 1944 Act, i.e. primary and secondary education, the replacement of old schools, the expansion of higher education, new priorities for different schemes under the Act and the expansion of teacher training for all these purposes.'

Below: Classroom entertainment at Victoria Road school, Edlington, during the mid-1950s.

Above and below: Outdoor activities at Victoria Road school, Edlington, in the mid-1950s.

On the climbing apparatus at Victoria Road school, Edlington in the mid-1950s.

Dancing round the Maypole at Victoria Road school, Edlington, in the mid-1950s.

The last train at Edlington Halt on Saturday 8 September 1951.

First-aid workers at Yorkshire Main colliery; note the pit props in the background. Tommy Hawker is on the left in the middle row.

Main Road, Edlington, looking towards Warmsworth. Woodcock's business premises are on the left, and the Co-op can be seen in the distance. On 20 June 1913 the *Doncaster Chronicle* stated: 'One of the most imposing buildings in the village are the fine premises of the Doncaster Co-operative Stores. Up to the present there has been very little competition in trade.' Dyson's business premises are off-centre to the right.

A similar view to the one above, but taken a little later, and perhaps showing the rise in motorized transport.

Edlington Methodist church at the corner of Main Avenue and Prince's Crescent. The chapel was opened in March 1925, the first minister being the Revd Harry Collinson.

View along Edlington Lane showing the Billiard Hall and York Hotel. The York Hotel was formerly owned by the Yorks Land Development Co. Ltd.

Above and below: Weighing nearly 15 tons each and powered by 100hp motors, two of the most powerful diesel locomotives to work underground on haulage at Yorkshire Main Colliery, Edlington, were lowered separately down one of the shafts in steel girder 'cradles' on Saturday 5 August 1950. They brought the total number of diesels working underground at the colliery to fourteen—the twelve already working underground at the pit were of 65hp. The two locomotives were run along a temporary railway line to the side of the shaft. Then began the task of fitting the first into its steel girder 'sling'. Inch by inch, under the direction of Bert Hall, the colliery engineer, the heavy diesel was 'persuaded' by workmen, using levers and manpower, into its temporary cradle. The cage was removed from the winding rope and the cable attached to the diesel's 'sling'. Ready for its 840-yard journey down the shaft, the locomotive was left while engineers checked on the winding engine and brakes.

View along Broomhouse Lane, extending between Edlington Lane and Springwell Lane.

The junction of Main Avenue and Edlington Lane. The business premises on the right include those of grocer and confectioner A. Spargo and Hutchinson the tobacconist. Across the road is the shop of dry-cleaners Clarks of Retford, and standing adjacent is a gents' hairdressing outlet.

Victoria Road school fishing club, *c.*1960. From left to right, back row: ? Bucknall, -?-, G. Fettis, Geoff Richards, teacher Martin Henry, Les Holmes, ? Fisher, Brian Lowe. Front row: ? Fox, -?-, Ian Brannan, Paul Drury.

Victoria Road school pupils, *c.*1960. From left to right, back row: Paul Blackwell, T. Wake, -?-, ? Faulkner, Dave Daniels, John Sutherland, George Ingram, teacher Mr Heppinstall. Middle row: Doug Barber, -?-, Roy Rowbotham, Steve Brown, M. Troth, -?-, Brian Lowe, ? Thorpe. Front row: ? Faulkner, Alan Taylor, -?-, -?-, Gary Allen, -?-, ? Pigeon.

Yorkshire Main sidings box. All the lines in the area along with the box have since been removed.

A scene at the Yorkshire Main Cricket Club annual prizegiving, held in the Welfare, c1957. Those depicted include Albert Allen, Billy Gough, Keith Thornycroft, Bill Barnes, Sammy Key, Andy Gough, Jack Cross, Ted Cross, and Eric Smith.

Edlington comprehensive school 4XB pupils, around November 1967. From left to right, back row: -?-, ? Leslie, ? Holmes, -?-, Peter Tuffrey, Dennis Kelman, Tom Ford, David Daniels. Third row: ? Kitchen, Alan Brown, Ian Jack, Billy Lang, -?-, -?-, Gary Allen. Second row: Melvin Holdsworth, -?-, George Ingram, Terry Doran, John Corby, Alan Taylor, Ian Peate, Stan Watson. Front row: Ralph Robinson, Tony Swift, -?-, teacher Alan Hampson, -?-, -?-, -?-.

Edlington comprehensive school pupils, around November 1967. From left to right, back row: -?-, Richard Childs, Barry Mee, Susan Head, David Birkinshaw. Third row: -?-, Geoff Allen, Ian Peate, David Shaw, Ronald Allen, -?-. Second row: -?-, John Williams, ? Boltrukiewicz, Des Ackroyd, Paul Blackwell. Front row: Lorraine Turner, Marilyn Rolston, Anne Smith, teacher David Burnett, -?-, Angela Clarke, Fay Mitchell.

Scenes at Yorkshire Main colliery on the retirement of 'pit poet' George Dungworth (holding pick and shovel), c.1980.

Above and below: The *Doncaster Chronicle* of 23 March 1923 carried a sketch 'of the building proposed to be erected at Edlington as the Miners' Welfare Scheme', which was subsequently erected. The newspaper also gave the following description: 'It takes the form of an Institute, with a concert hall holding 400, billiard room, smoking room, etc. The grounds will be used for football, cricket, and other recreational purposes. The cost will be over £6,000.' The architect was T. Sydney Johnson, Doncaster, and the building contractors were Thomson & Dixon, Doncaster. The two pictures here show the demolition of the building in the 1970s.

Visit of National Coal Board chief Derek Ezra to Yorkshire Main Colliery.

Dismantling the railway bridge over Edlington Lane, during 1970.

Clashes between pickets and police during the 1984–85 miners' strike at Edlington. In April 1984, a few weeks after the national pit strike had commenced, Jim McFarlane, leader of Doncaster Council, called into question police tactics in dealing with the miners. He claimed there were examples of police activity which went beyond what people in South Yorkshire had come to expect. There was a thin dividing line between maintaining law and order and the suppression of the liberty of individuals; he said. 'My fear is that once crossed, that dividing line will disappear. Examples of police action which are now appearing cause me mounting concern. The South Yorkshire Police have an enviable record for policing our community by consensus and I have been in the forefront of those who have voiced their appreciation of that fine record.'

In April 1984, Councillor McFarlane also added that a Democracy Day had been declared as an expression of concern about increasing Government control in communities. 'I hope the South Yorkshire Police Force is alive to the danger of being seen as an integral arm of that tendency.'

Above and below: More clashes between pickets and police during the 1984–85 miners' strike. In reply to criticism of their handling of the miners' strike, police leaders vowed that no political pressure would change their policing of pickets. The Police Federation county chairman Bob Lax attacked the county council and South Yorkshire police committee, who held an inquiry into the police handling of the miners' strike. He said that at one meeting of the police committee, relationships had reached an all-time low, as county councillors made wild and sometimes hysterical allegations about the police 'bully boys' refusing to allow miner to talk to miner. 'It is time the officers who have to perform picket-line duties had a bit of moral support for the lousy job they were having to do to in trying to maintain the democratic rights of people who want to work.' He told a meeting attended by members of the police committee that the police service 'is non-political and will remain non-political'.

Above: A picket is given a 'helping' hand by police at Yorkshire Main.

Below: Britain's longest and bitterest strike ended on 5 March 1985, a day short of the anniversary of the NCB's closure plan announcement on 6 March 1984. After a strife-torn three-hour meeting, NUM president Arthur Scargill was noted as declaring: 'The strike is over, but the dispute over pit closures and job losses goes on.' The picture shows Yorkshire Main miners proudly returning to work.

Yorkshire Main Cricket Club members. From left to right, back row: Eric Smith, Bob Gater, Peter Barker, George Brealey, Peter Smith, John Gregson, Roy Yeomans, Jimmy Henry, Neil Warnes, Mick Smith, Jim Ramage, Ken Allen and Martin Henry. Front row: Alick Ramage, Martin Gregson, Melvin Hartley, Derek Ainsworth, Gerry Wakelin, Gordon Leyland, Lester Ainsworth.

Opposite, above and below: Demolition of the No. 2 shaft (up-cast) winding tower at Yorkshire Main. No. 1 shaft engine house is in the background. In December 1991, a memorial to the men of Yorkshire Main and their families over seven decades was erected. Generations of Edlington men worked, were injured and even died at the pit upon which the village depended. It all ended in 1985 when the colliery was closed in the aftermath of the year-long miners' strike. A pit wheel, salvaged from the old colliery site, now stands in silent tribute on a plinth outside the Officials' Club. An inscription on a plaque says it all: 'Yorkshire Main Colliery stood on this site from 1910 to 1985, a tribute and memorial to all who died in accidents here or whose lives were shortened by disease, injury or sickness, and to their families. Their contribution to the energy needs of the nation and the developments of Edlington must not be forgotten.' Edlington Town Council Officials' Club and developers of the old colliery site had co-operated in the memorial's erection.

SITE CLEARANCE
LINDLEY EXCAVATIONS
BARNSLEY
S. YORKS.
0226 758849
CRUSHING
EXCAVATIONS
PLANT HIRE

Above and below: Housing development on the Yorkshire Main Colliery site.

Another Development by
YORKSHIRE
METROPOLITAN
PROPERTIES LTD
TELEPHONE (03021) 310606

Bramall
Design BUILD
From concept to creation
TELEPHONE
(0302) 341030

Two

Maltby

In the booklet *Maltby and its Residential Advantages and Industrial Activities* (undated), it is stated: 'The bracing air from the surrounding hills, the numerous woods and open spaces and the plentiful supplies of sunshine, help to make it an exceedingly healthy place.' Before the coming of the colliery, Maltby was essentially a community in farming and other associated rural trades. Also, it has a history which goes back to before the Norman Conquest. This picture shows Woodlea, Maltby.

Left: Interior view of St Bartholomew's church, Maltby. The church was once described as a 'small and rather mean building forming a remarkable contrast to the once magnificent church of the Cistercians,' who had established themselves in its vicinity. On the rafters of the roof are painted the names of some early benefactors.

Below: The church of St Bartholomew, Maltby, comprises nave, chancel, north and south aisles, tower and spire. The church was rebuilt in 1859, except for the tower.

Opposite above: In 1924, Maltby's population had grown to such an extent, as a result of the mining community being established, that Maltby Parish Council was superseded by Maltby Urban District Council. In the MUDC's Silver Jubilee souvenir booklet, it was claimed: '[Since 1924] the township has made excellent use of its increased powers. It has been fortunate in having had as its leaders ambitious men who, in the interests of the community, knew how to take full advantage of their opportunities.' The view here shows Maltby from Hooton Hill.

MALTBY CHURCH.

Another view of Maltby from Hooton Levitt. Maltby's population in 1901 was 716; 1911, 1700; 1921, 7,657; 1931, 10,013; 1935, 10,610. In the past, Maltby has known a number of variations in the spelling of the name: Malby, Maultby, Maultbie, Maltebi, Maltegbie, Maleybie.

Maltby vicarage. The rectors of Maltby are recorded from 1230 to 1369, and the vicars from 1240 to the present day.

Street scene at Maltby. Situated in the extreme south-west of the West Riding of Yorkshire, close to the Nottinghamshire and Derbyshire borders, the town of Maltby stands some 400 feet above sea level and about mid-way between the industrial centres of Rotherham and Doncaster.

Above and below: Looking towards High Street, the two views show Makins Hill, with a well in the foreground, prior to road developments in the area. An article in the *Doncaster Chronicle* of 16 March 1928, headed 'Disappearing Maltby', stated: 'Makins Hill cottages are now chiefly unoccupied, having been condemned as unfit for habitation; they will shortly be demolished for road improvements.' The large house, however, dominating both pictures, still stands today, though in an unoccupied state.

Another view of Makins Hill, facing High Street, where the monument on the right was erected in memory of Dr William Henry Crosby by his second wife, Mary Jane and their children. Crossley, according to an inscription, 'was fatally injured near this spot on St Paul's Day, 1900.' It also added: 'At eventide it shall be light.' Following road improvements the monument was moved to a slightly different position in the thoroughfare.

Street scene at Maltby.

E.1.5.43-53 The Hall, Maltby.

The Hall, Maltby, which was occupied for most of the nineteenth century by the Rolleston family. The Hall has since been demolished, with Maltby Comprehensive school now marking the site.

The Terrace, Maltby Hall. On the death of Revd George Rolleston, in 1868, the estate passed into the hands of the Schofields of Sand Hall, near Howden, and the Revd Philip Schofield went to reside at the Hall. For a time the Hall served the purpose of a ladies' school, before being purchased by W. Mackenzie Smith, son of F.P. Smith of Barnes Hall. Mackenzie Smith, who married a sister of Earl Fitzwilliam, resided at the hall for several years.

The garden front, Hooton Levitt Hall. For much of the eighteenth and nineteenth centuries, Hooton Levitt Hall was tenanted by the Hoyle family. One member, W.F. Hoyle (1801–1886), was a noted lawyer. The Hall has since been demolished. At one time, the Lord of the Manor and sole landowner of Hooton Levitt, lying half-a-mile south west of Maltby, was Lt-Col. Arnold. The population at the beginning of the twentieth century was seventy-six.

Above: The Hall, Hooton Levitt.

Opposite above: In October 1907, the Maltby Main Colliery Company, a subsidiary of the Sheepbridge Coal & Iron Company Ltd, began sinking No. 1 shaft, 20ft finished diameter, reaching the Barnsley Bed, the only seam worked, at a depth of 820 yards on 13 January 1911. The fastest rate of sinking was 18 yards a week. No. 2 shaft, also 20ft finished diameter, was commenced in September 1907 and completed in July 1910. The Barnsley Bed was reached on 18 June 1910. The picture here shows pit sinkers at Maltby Main.

The Maltby Main colliery was the scene of a terrible explosion in the early hours of Monday morning, 20 August 1911. Three miners lost their lives, and a number of men who went to their aid and rescue had narrow escapes. The men killed were Horace Jepson (aged twenty-six), Tom Turton (twenty-eight) and John Butler (thirty-one). All the men were single and lived at the Model Village Maltby. They died from burns, the bodies being found badly charred. The deceased, with twenty-one others, went to work at 10 p.m. the previous night. The reason for so few men being on the night shift was the stoppage caused by a railway strike. The men were engaged in driving No. 4 heading in No. 2 shaft, 300 yards from the pit bottom. About 3 a.m. a slight explosion was heard.

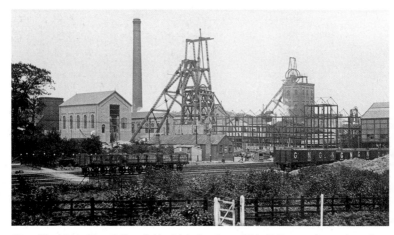

Above: The *Maltby Main Colliery Golden Jubilee* brochure, 1911–1961, states that in the early days there were between 300 and 400 men winning coal by hand and filling it into tubs. 'Large quantities of industrial, gas and coking coals, as well as the world-famous "London Brights" were extracted and by 1935 a million tons per annum was being mined.' The colliery grew in size and importance, and labour was attracted not only from the local villages but from as far afield as Derbyshire, Durham, Lancashire and Ireland. The village of Maltby grew rapidly and the mining community shared in the prosperity and employment.

In 1925, the first pit-head baths were constructed at the colliery. Two years later, the colliery passed into the control of the Denaby & Cadeby Main Collieries Ltd, and in 1935 became more closely embodied in the Amalgamated Denaby Collieries Ltd, a powerful and enlightened concern, which had under its control Denaby, Cadeby, Dinnington and Rossington collieries. The great experience which Amalgamated Denaby Collieries Ltd had of mining in South Yorkshire, ensured the continued progress of Maltby.

Opposite below: The screens at Maltby Colliery. At a shareholders' meeting in July 1911, Maurice Deacon, chairman and managing director of the Maltby Main Colliery Company, reported that the erection of plant was proceeding satisfactorily. The winding part of the plant was laid out for raising 5,000 to 6,000 tons per day, and if trade warranted them raising more than 2,500 or 3,000 tons it would be necessary to increase the screens and the sidings in order to deal with the larger quantity.

A view along Blyth Road, looking towards Rotherham Road, with the White Swan public house in the distance on the left. In an advertisement dating from the mid-1930s, it is mentioned that the inn, formerly owned by Mappins Masborough Brewery Co., was the oldest and most comfortable hotel in the town. It had also served the public throughout the reign of five King Georges, from George I in August 1714 to George V in 1935.

A street scene with the Tinsley to Bawtry turnpike on the left, and the Rotherham to Barnby Moor turnpike on the right. In subsequent years, extensive road improvements were made in the vicinity.

Maltby station, which was 1¼ miles east of the village on the Doncaster and Shireoaks branch of the South Yorkshire Joint Lines Committee.

The Queen's Hotel at the Muglet Lane/Tickhill Road junction, Maltby.

Another disaster occurred at Maltby colliery on 28 July 1923. A gob fire (spontaneous combustion of waste behind the coalface) had been discovered in the Low East District; during sealing-off operations there was a violent explosion, and twenty-eight men lost their lives. These views show Herbert Smith, President of the Miners' Federation of Great Britain, meeting with local union officials and relatives of the disaster victims.

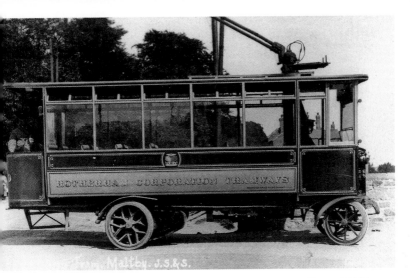

Above and below: The Maltby trolleybus route, extending between Broom Top and Maltby, was opened on 30 October 1912. At the time, the route of 4¾ miles was the longest trolleybus route in the country. The twenty-two-seat vehicles were painted in red and yellow and divided into two compartments. One of these provided accommodation for sixteen smokers. The route was declared open by Ald. D.L. Winter, Chairman of the Electric Light and Tramways Committee. At one time it was noted there was an excellent trolleybus service from Rotherham (College Street) every half hour from 4.40 a.m. to 11 p.m., through Wickersley and Bramley. The return fare was 10d.

Trolley accident on the Maltby route.

Vehicle no. 39 pictured on the Maltby route.

Opposite above: A rural scene at Maltby where the lighting of streets was formerly carried out by the Maltby & Bramley Gas Co. (offices in Rotherham Road). The electricity for domestic lighting, heating and power purposes was supplied by the Yorkshire Electric Power Company. One of the buildings on the left once offered 'refreshments for cyclists'. The *Doncaster Chronicle* of 16 March 1928 mentioned: 'The old coffee house on the Low Road [Blyth Road], well-known to visitors fifty or more years ago and now a grocer's shop, is soon to be pulled down for road widening, and there are other ancient houses near which are to share the same fate.'

The Don John public house on High Street. In *A History of Maltby* produced by the WEA, 1968, it is mentioned: 'The second oldest surviving inn is the Don John with the present structure being built in 1911 when Maltby's population was beginning to increase because of the colliery development. The previous inn on this site had been named after the winner of the 1838 St Leger stakes at Doncaster ... Whether this was a new inn built in this year or whether it was the renaming of either the George and Dragon or the Yellow Lion is not at present known, but neither of them are mentioned in the directories after 1838, while the newcomers are the Don John and the Scarborough Arms.'

Above and below: In June 1910, it was claimed that the opening of Maltby Colliery would not add materially to the population of the old village. The reason for this was that a new village was being laid out in anticipation of the coming of the colliers, between the old village and the pit-head. Some 400 houses were projected, and a considerable number of these were completed or well on the road to completion. The site was being laid out on 'model village' lines, a central space being reserved for a village green or recreation ground. The housing question at Maltby was not being tackled by the Colliery Company in the same way as had been done at Brodsworth, but the Company were making themselves responsible for 'seeing that their employees would be comfortably housed.' On the site in question, a local builder, Mr Mollekin, was putting up the houses to the approval of the Company who were leasing them for a term of years for the accommodation of the miners. The situation of the village, right on the top of the hill, was a good one 'from the hygienic standpoint', and although the village itself might not have the natural attractions which the existence of growing trees gave to Woodlands, it was argued that the houses themselves were better and more solidly built than at the latter place. In short, they were an improvement on those met with in colliery villages of the old type.

Above: View along Millindale. On 17 August 1911 the *Doncaster Chronicle* reported on the failure of Maltby builder Herbert Mollekin who had been involved with construction work in the model village: 'The Official receiver stated that proofs already sent in caused the deficiency as estimated by the debtor to rise another £4,409. That amount included a sum of … £1,512 damages claimed to have been sustained by breach of an agreement with the Maltby Main Colliery Co. Ltd, for the construction of houses at Maltby Model village.'

Below: In 1923 there were 7,000 inhabitants at Maltby. By the 1950s the population had doubled. But, unlike many South Yorkshire mining villages, Maltby is not dominated by the mine, which is over a mile from the centre of the village. At one time, the miners ran their own bus service from the village to the colliery, possibly the only scheme of its kind in the country. The men paid 2s 6d a week for the service, which also included the delivery of their concessionary coal.

Above and below: In an article headed 'Maltby's £10,000 New School—Palatial Premises—First on the Quadrangle Principle and Finest in the Country' the *Doncaster Chronicle* of 31 May 1912 reported: 'The handsome new buildings which the West Riding County Council have just completed at the very heart of the new mining modern village are the finest in the country ... The front elevation of the boys' department [the entrance is seen in the picture below] faces the Worksop Road, overlooking the picturesque Craggs and affording a glimpse of delightful scenery, and hill and dale ... The school buildings are arranged on four sides of a square, in the centre of which is a large green lawn beautifully turfed and surrounded by asphalt ... Each room is fitted with a picture rail and with museum cases, the contents of which can be seen both from the class rooms and from the corridors. The ventilation throughout the school is absolutely perfect ... The new school will be opened with befitting ceremonial in a few days' time and among those who are expected to attend the proceedings is Sir Charles Nicholson M.P.'

Above: View along Rotherham Road, Maltby, during the trolleybus era.

Below: View along Rolleston Avenue, from Rotherham Road. Maltby's Silver Jubilee souvenir booklet notes that on 21 December 1926, thirty-six houses were completed in the Rolleston Avenue Council Housing Scheme. George Rolleston, MD FRS, Linacre Professor of Physiology in the University of Oxford, was born at Maltby on 30 July 1829. He died at Oxford on 16 June 1881. The Revd George Rolleston, after whom the council houses and an old people's home were named, occupied Maltby Hall for a period during the nineteenth century.

Another view along Rotherham Road, Maltby, during the trolleybus era.

View along Maltby High Street. In the past it was stated that Maltby possessed a number 'of capital shops wherein a variety of needs are supplied. One does not, of course, look for department stores in a place of this size.'

Opposite above: New church, Model Village, Maltby. The dedication of the new Maltby Mission church was made by the Archbishop of York on 16 May 1912. The church was one of the first of eight new mission buildings to be erected under the South Yorkshire Coalfield church extension scheme. The total cost was £2,000.

Interior view of New church, Model Village, Maltby. The church was built by Messrs Sprakes & Sons of Doncaster to the designs prepared by F. Norman D. Masters, based upon the Italian Romanesque or Lombardy Architecture, and had seating accommodation for 400 people. The first Curate-in-Charge was the Rev. Douglas H. Crick.

Muglet Lane, facing north with Morrell Street out of view to the left. One of the gabled buildings in the distance carries a 1912 date stone, the other one formerly belonged to Millards. The Picture House on the right no longer fulfils its original function, being currently occupied by the Grand Kitchen Warehouse.

Blyth Road facing the town centre. Interestingly, a second gable has since been added to the building on the right (now the Melton Court Nursing Home), since the photograph was taken.

Above and below: The *Maltby Main Colliery Golden Jubilee 1911–1961* booklet mentions: 'Today the large-scale £3 million reconstruction scheme both on the surface and underground is almost completed. The most modern types of electric winders, one of which is capable of lifting 480 tons of coal per hour, are in operation and a new and highly efficient coal preparation plant has been built.' The top picture shows No. 2 shaft surface reconstruction while the one below shows shaft No. 1 surface reconstruction taking place on 30 July 1958.

Above and below: One of the main difficulties at Maltby was that the seam of coal ran on a downward gradient from the pit bottom, making it impossible to introduce locomotive haulage from the working districts to the latter area. To overcome this problem it was decided to deepen the shafts by 50 yards to a new winding level. This allowed the construction of reasonably level roadways to the working districts and the introduction of mine-cars. Powerful diesel and electric battery locomotives hauled the loaded mine cars to the pit bottom and there was radio communication between the drivers of these locomotives and the various loading points. The two pictures here show the scene underground at Maltby during the 1950s.

Above: By the early 1960s, there were seven operating faces and one training face, and of these, six were power-loaded; Huwood slicer machines being used. Some idea of the progress made could be deduced from the fact that, with a labour force of 2,088 in 1948, 682,702 tons of coal were produced. In 1960, with the labour force reduced to 2,011, the output was increased to 820,612 tons. The above picture shows one of the underground battery locomotives.

Below: A five-coach train hauled by a Class B1 locomotive pauses at Maltby on 11 May 1952 to enable the 200 members of the Railway Correspondence and Travel Society and friends to take photographs and inspect the station, which was one of only three stations on the South Yorkshire Joint Railway. A passenger service between Doncaster and Shireoaks, which operated from 1910 to 1929, used to call at Maltby. At the time of the photograph, the station still catered for occasional special or excursion trains.

Left and below: A new winding tower, enabling Maltby colliery to become South Yorkshire's first pit producing 2 million tons a year, was taking shape in double quick time in July 1982. A 230ft tower was constructed in a total of twenty-two days, with men working twenty-four hours a day, seven days a week. Using conventional methods, the work could have taken up to two years to complete. The National Coal Board's chief mining engineer in the South Yorkshire area, Jack Pocock, explained: 'The tower is rising between four and six inches every hour.' The tower was part of a £130 million project to tap about 50 million tons of coal in the Parkgate and Thorncliffe seams at the mine. The seams had not previously been worked from Maltby. Once work on constructing the winding tower had come to an end—and some 11,000 tons of concrete had gone into its structure—work was to recommence on the shaft-sinking. The fan drift had been driven and the first 45m of the main shaft had already been sunk.

Right and below: On completion of the development work, the shaft would be 1,000m deep—one of the deepest in Yorkshire. And, at 8m in diameter, the new shaft was to be the biggest in the country. It was to be fitted with four 23-ton capacity skips to raise coal for the whole mine. The skips, like huge buckets, were to be drawn up and down the shaft by two 4,000hp winding engines mounted in the new tower. At this time, it was proclaimed that Maltby had sufficient reserves in the Swallow Wood and Haigh Moor seams to last beyond the year 2000, ensuring the jobs of 2,000 local men well into the twenty-first century. Included in the 1982 investment project was a new coal preparation plant. It would clean and grade coal to meet exacting requirements of future customers from industry, power stations and the steel industry.

Maltby colliery's record-breaking 'driving' team, which made 160m in five days and 230.5m in one week—a European record. The team is pictured in June 1996.

Three

Warmsworth

Children posing on Common Lane, Warmsworth. Those identified include, from left to right: -?-, Irene Morton, -?-, -?-, -?-, Pauline Marks, -?-, Hilary Harper, Pat Wilson, Sandra Sanderson, -?-, -?-, -?-, Valerie Large, Gillian Wood, Mary Lawrence, Gillian Thorley.

Warmsworth cricket team, c. 1910. This picture surely epitomizes the almost universally accepted idea of what a village cricket team looked like. From left to right, back row: George Linill, Vonda Patrick, Jack Lewis, George Longley, Charlie Aston, Jack Barker Jnr, Jack Barker Snr. Middle row: Arthur Oldfield, Dick Firth, Jack Guest, Will Longley, Tom Ashmore. Front row: Bill Drabble, Tom Barker.

Warmsworth Cricket Club decided to make 1987 their centenary year, though it was stated there was sufficient evidence to suggest there was a cricket club in Warmsworth much earlier than 1887. A note in the local newspaper from 1850 records a game against near neighbours Sprotbrough, yet there was no evidence to indicate whether there was continuity up to 1887. Cricket matches in the early years were 'friendlies' against other village clubs, and this was the pattern until 1926.

Low Road East, looking towards the junction with Common Lane/Glebe Street. The entrance to Warmsworth Hall can be seen in the distance. At one time a Mr Jack Guest lived in one of the houses and sold fruit and vegetables. The Drabble family occupied the cottage adjacent the Hall entrance. The bell in the tower, just out of view, was tolled at weddings and funerals and to announce other events at the old church.

Low Road West, looking towards Quaker Lane. Two of the cottages on the right were demolished, c.1960. The arched entrance once led to a shop and two other cottages. The shop was kept for a period by the Merrills family.

A group of locals pose for the camera.

This picture is reputedly an early view of Warmsworth Football Club.

Opposite above: High Road, Warmsworth, in the days of trams. Just beyond the tram is the old pinfold on Calf's Head Lane, now Tenter Road. The tram route was extended from Oswin Avenue, Balby, to Warmsworth on 4 February 1915. Work on laying the track had started in October 1914. An opening ceremony was conducted by Councillor P. Stirling, Chairman of the Electricity and Tramways Committee. Trams terminated outside the Cecil and Battie Wrightson Arms until 1919 when a short spur was constructed along Edlington Lane, after which cars stopped beside the Co-operative Society's building. Trams ceased running along the route on 26 July 1931.

High Road, Warmsworth, the picture taken before the coming of trams. The post office formerly occupied the house on the east end of the row of cottages. The Harris, Pinkney, Spinks and English families once lived in the cottages.

Above left: Local resident Jessie Birkinshaw posing as Britannia.

Above right: Jessie Birkinshaw (later Drabble) in fancy dress.

Below: Edlington Lane with W. Brown's General Store, on the right.

Jessie Birkinshaw and members of the Patrick family and friends pose in fancy dress.

A view taken from the Edlington Lane/Sheffield Road junction, looking west. Wrightson and Cecil Avenues are in the distance on the left.

Henry A. Plowright's blacksmith's shop on High Road, Warmsworth. Henry's sign on the front of the building states that he was a shoeing and general smith. It also gives the following information: 'Farm implements made and repaired, all orders neatly and promptly executed.'

Above left: The bell tower, Warmsworth. In *St Peter's Church, Warmsworth* by Hey and Magilton (1983), it is noted: 'The parish church, 1km distant from the village centre, on the eastern parish boundary, is unusually sited, and until the completion of the present [White] church, services were announced in the village by a bell attached to a tower of unknown date at the end of the parsonage croft near the gates of Warmsworth Hall.'

Above right: A gathering near the Cecil and Battie-Wrightson Arms.

Opposite below: During February 1911, one of many changes that were soon to affect rural Warmsworth occurred with the closing of the old village inn and the opening of a new one. The new establishment was described as an attractive building of red brick, the upper storeys overlaid with stucco. Local builder and ex-Councillor Wortley was responsible for erecting the building at the junction of four roads to Edlington, Conisbrough, Sprotbrough, and Doncaster. The house was christened the Cecil and Battie Wrightson Arms (taking the two surnames of land owner Lady Isabella Battie-Wrightson, *née* Cecil), contrasting with the modest title of the Barrel, under which the old inn had traded. The new house, which opened on Monday 13 February 1911, had a seven-day licence. George Guest was the genial host and tenant. The old house—The Barrel Inn, was a two-storey terrace of rooms, one room only in width, the result of rebuildings and additions from time to time. At one time, it was a well-known roadside hostel, but since the road was diverted, it became an out-of-the-way and secluded house. The Barrel was for many years occupied by the Guests, and for a similar number of years was closed to the public on the Sabbath.

Rear view of Edlington Lane, looking south-east, *c*.1930. In later years, the east side of Wrightson Avenue was built on the open space where the two children are playing.

View along Cecil Avenue, *c*.1930, looking towards Edlington.

The *Last Post* is sounded during the unveiling of the war memorial at Warmsworth on Saturday 17 September 1921. The memorial, which had cost about £150, was made by Tyas & Guest of Swinton. The war memorial was subsequently moved to the new burial ground. The names of those who fell in the Second World War were added to the eastern side of the memorial, while the names of the four victims of the Warmsworth air crash of 27 February 1940 were inscribed on the western side.

Posing for the camera along Wrightson Avenue, Warmsworth.

Road sweepers pose
for the camera while
working on Low Road.

Sheffield Road, with the Doncaster Co-operative Society's premises on the left. The branch was opened on Wednesday evening, 2 July, 1913. Councillor C. Wightman, president, presided at a public tea concert and meeting in celebration of the event. Facing the Battie-Wrightson Arms public house, the stores were expected to serve a projected large population, in the wake of the opening of the new Yorkshire Main colliery, at Edlington. The other districts it was to serve comprised Sprotbrough, Levitt Hagg, and Cusworth. There was a grocery stores, a butchery department, and a house at the side. It was a two-storey building, the rooms over the shops being used as store-rooms. They had cost £2,000 to build. A large number sat down to tea, and the attendance was considerably increased for the concert and meeting. Councillor Wightman gave an address, during the course of which he stated that the Doncaster Society contained 14,047 members, and the share capital amounted to £141,255. Several members of the committee addressed the meeting.

The Warmsworth tramway extension was constructed largely to serve the Yorkshire Main colliery, a mile down Edlington Lane (on the left). The tram's route indicator, in the above photograph, as well as denoting that the vehicle was working on a cross-town service to Beckett Road, helps to date the picture to sometime between 1915 (when the Warmsworth extension opened) and 1917 when cross-town services ceased. The failure to extend the route as far as Edlington encouraged private motor bus competition and the Corporation was forced to run its own motor bus service from 1923.

Warmsworth Mill Lane school group. From left to right, back row: -?-, -?-, -?-, George Smith, -?-, -?-, Noel Lewis. Third row: Bob Merrion, -?-, -?-, Mary Kendall, Bob Wheeldon, Doris Barton, -?-, Mary Wood, Roma Robinson. Second row: Eric Kevern, Doris Baker, Eric Spencer, -?-, Horace Pick, Harvey Dennis, Charlie Smith. Front row: Eric Goddard, -?-, Harry Smith, John Lewis, Robert Sanderson, -?-.

Warmsworth Mill Lane school group. From left to right, back row: -?-, -?-, Harry Parnham, Kendall, -?-, -?-, -?-. Third row: Frank Lawrence, -?-, -?-, ? Cook, ? Wood, ? Pick. Second row: Bill Lawrence, -?-, -?-, -?-. Front row: -?-, -?-, Eric Thompson.

From left to right, back row: -?-, -?-, ? Nicholson, Mary Butlin, Harold Southall, Arthur Merrion, ? Dent, -?-, Roger Brown. Third row: -?-, -?-, -?-, Eric Goddard, -?-, -?-, -?-, -?-. Second row: Ralph Richardson, Joan Wraith, Roy Pickering, -?-, Joyce Cook, -?-, Eddie Severs, -?-, -?-. Front row: -?-, Barbara Spencer, Marjorie Dennis, -?-, -?-, George Severs, -?-.

Edlington Lane, looking towards Cecil Avenue on the left. The Graceholme Social Working Men's Club and Institute is also on the extreme left in the picture. The club was formed in 1936.

Warmsworth Low Road school. From left to right, back row: ? Havercroft, Jack Sharpe, Harry Dennis, Reg Hill, -?-, -?-, Owen Stacey, Eric Goddard. Fourth row: Phil Sanderson, -?-, -?-, Stella Stacey, Marjorie Hill, Joyce Langley, Eddie Plowright, -?-, Peggy Shaw. Third row: Teacher Miss McGowan, Jim Cruncorn, Gerald Cook, Alice Spink, -?-, Enid Parkin, Ivy Parkin, Ronald Lunn, Wilson, teacher Miss Laurie. Second row: -?-, -?-, -?-, Harold Holmes, Eric Thompson, Robert Sanderson, Jim Cunningham, ? Holmes, Cathy Cunningham. Front row: -?-, -?-, Ralph Richardson, Eric Pick, -?-.

Above: Mill Lane junior school, viewed from Mill Lane. When the author attended this school, the main building on the right was used as an assembly hall/dining room. The small building to the left included a staff room and the Headmaster's/Headmistress's study. During the early 1960s, a Miss Eagles and later Bob Woodward occupied the latter room.

Below: Low Road West, looking west. The cottages on the left have since been 'modernized'. Over the wall and out of view to the right is Warmsworth House.

Above and below: Local historian John Tomlinson, writing in 1876, said that the parish church of St Peter, Warmsworth, had been rebuilt some seventy years earlier. White's *Directory of the West Riding* stated that the new church had been in existence for about twenty-five years. In turn, this building was replaced by another edifice, known locally as the White Church, in Warmsworth Road during 1942.

Interior of the old St Peter's church.

Above: The choir posing outside the old St Peter's church. Identifiable in the group are Ernie Parkin, a Mr Parnham and a Mr Windle.

Opposite above: On Saturday afternoon, 25 February 1933, the new burial ground provided by the Parish Council of Warmsworth was officially opened and consecrated. The ornamental gates at the entrance formerly adorned the Doncaster Road entrance to Sprotbrough Park, the home of the Copleys, which was demolished in the 1920s. The whole scheme of re-setting the gates to their new purpose was satisfactorily harmonized by the building of a low stone wall with iron railings surmounting it. The stone for this came from an old wall at Westfield Park, Balby, demolished for a road improvement scheme.

View along Low Road West. The 1953 *Warmsworth Coronation Celebrations* souvenir book states that the old village of Warmsworth, including the hall, is built in the main from Warmsworth stone obtained no doubt from the disused quarry at Edlington Lane, but during the eighteenth century, Warmsworth stone had a further usefulness, being known far and wide as a component of the best lime for soil treatment. The woman on the right has been identified as Mrs Symmons, a resident of one of the cottages.

Girls posing on the roller in the old cricket ground.

12-14 Glebe St. Warmsworth. JSaS.

Glebe Street looking towards High Road, with the Belfry on the left. Much infilling with new properties and the redevelopment of existing ones has taken place along the thoroughfare since the picture was taken. In the Warmsworth Coronation Celebrations 1953 souvenir booklet, it is mentioned: 'Glebe Street no doubt derives its name from the old Glebe, Moot Hall or Tythe Barn. The Glebe, or Moot Hall, was the local place where tenants of the Lords of the Manor paid their annual rents to the Overlord in kind; such rent comprising produce of the land held under the Lord of the Manor.'

Children posing on Common Lane. Amongst those identified are, from left to right, back row: -?-, -?-, -?-, Gillian Thorley, -?-, David Bee, -?-, -?-, John Body, Pat Wilson, Sandra Sanderson. Front row: -?-, -?-, Mary Lawrence, -?-, -?-, Hilary Harper, teacher, Gillian Wood, Valerie Large, -?-, Irene Morton, -?-, -?-.

Wrightson Avenue looking north towards Sheffield Road, c.1950. The scene is much different today with nearly every householder owning a motor vehicle.

Edlington Lane, looking towards Edlington and featuring grocer E. Knaggs' shop on the right. The shop still thrives today, though under different owners.

High Road, facing Doncaster, with the Beech Grove cash stores on the left. An advertisement in the centre of the picture for the Balby Windsor Cinema reveals that the films being shown there included *Indian Uprising* and *Desert Legion*.

On 25 May 1939, the *Doncaster Chronicle* stated that Doncaster would shortly have a modern church which would reflect the trends of modern architecture: 'a church which will not follow the traditional lines, but which will be built so as to make use of every inch of space. The [new] church of St Peter's [Warmsworth] is to adjoin the Rectory on a plot of land which has been given to the church by Mr Battie-Wrightson, of Cusworth Hall. The site provides for a parish hall as well as space for a churchyard. The architect was Captain C.M. Cooper of the firm of Messrs Brundell & Farran, Doncaster. The *Doncaster Chronicle* of 14 March 1940 showed a picture of the new church under construction. The foundation stone was laid by the Bishop of Sheffield (Dr L.S. Hunter) on 4 November 1939, on the occasion of his first visit to Doncaster.

During January 1941, it was announced that the exterior of the new church of St Peter at Warmsworth had been completed. After considerable delay, mainly owing to the difficulty of obtaining materials, the new church was consecrated by the Bishop of Sheffield on Saturday 28 March at 6 p.m. The church, which is in the form of a Greek basilica, was intended to serve a rapidly growing residential area. The provision of a new church for Warmsworth was projected about the time of the centenary of the parish, but the parochial church council felt unable to embark on so large a task, owing to the low resources of the parish. The Sheffield Diocesan Board of Finance, however, determined that the need was so exceptional as to justify their guaranteeing the capital outlay, part of which was to be repaid.

Warmsworth cricket team during the 1940s. From left to right, back row: Terry Webster, John Mellors, Harry Dennis, Frank Dixon, Harold ?, Charlie Pateman, Eric Wells. Front row: Laurence Waghorn, Harry Gleadall, Tommy Walters, Bob ?, ? Ward.

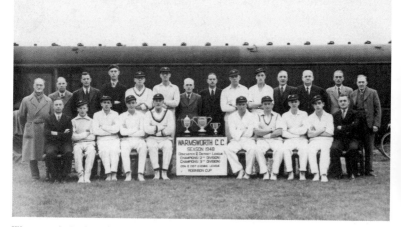

Warmsworth Cricket Club's first team, winners of the Second Division championship in 1948. From left to right, back row: ? Merrills (groundsman), ? Carter, Harry Wadsworth, Jim Robinson, J. Gale, E.Hoyle (chairman), W. Findlay (president), Ted Steel, Harold Wood, Eric Thompson, -?-, Sam Russon. Front row: Eric Wells, Dick Goodman, G. Jones, Dougie Turner, Tom Webster (captain), Bob Bates, Herbert Oldfield, Johnny Butler, Bob Webster, ? Aldred.

A view of Sheffield Road with the Cecil Hotel in the distance. The entrances to Wrightson and Cecil Avenues may be seen on the right. The approaching vehicle is a Pathfinder van.

On 19 August 1954, the *Doncaster Chronicle* stated that Warmsworth Cricket Club had a wonderful record of success in their twenty-eight years' existence in the Doncaster and District Cricket League, and in that time 'they have won five championships'. The 1950s team depicted here includes, from left to right, back row: Eddie Dixon, Brian Lowe, -?-, Carter, -?-. Front row: -?-, -?-, Geoff Norman, Harry Gleadall, Tommy Walters, Laurence Waghorn.

Above: A view of Cliff Crescent, Warmsworth, extending between Mill Lane and Tenter Lane.

Below: Beech Grove, facing north, with the Beech Grove cash stores just visible on the right. Interestingly, one of the signs on the building reads: 'Smoke Craven A will not affect your throat.'

Above and below: Following the death of V.M. Dowson of West Farm, Warmsworth, during the late 1950s, there was a sale of his agricultural machinery, and some of the items can be seen in these two pictures.

Left: View showing what is thought to be the first gala to be held on the sports ground, where the pipe band from Yorkshire Main colliery can be seen.

Below: A derelict stone quarry, off Edlington Lane, Warmsworth, was transformed into a garden park at a cost of more than £10,000 in August 1955. The official opening ceremony was performed by Alderman H.J. Bambridge, chairman of the West Riding County Council (he is pictured opening the gate). At the ceremony, he said more local authorities ought to become 'flower conscious'—more aware of the need for beautifying their town and village centres. At a dinner before the official opening, Mrs Noble, chairman of Doncaster Rural Council, had described how the quarry, formerly rat-infested, was offered to the Rural Council in 1950 for use as a tip. They decided, however, to develop it as a park.

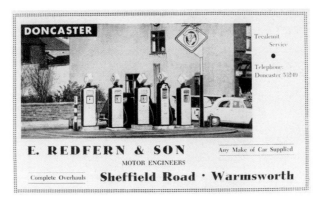

Above and below: In September 1959, a petition with 1,465 signatures was sent by Warmsworth Parish Council to the West Riding Rural District Council in support of garage owner W. Redfern, whose appeal was to be heard on 7 October. The appeal was against a Ministry of Transport refusal to grant permission for him to build a new garage and filling station alongside his existing premises at the Sheffield Road/Mill Lane junction, which were to be pulled down for road improvements. In May, the following year, it was announced that the new premises could be built, but W. Redfern would not be able to use them until he ceased using his existing premises. This was the decision of the Minister of Housing who granted an appeal by W. Redfern against the RDC's earlier decision refusing permission to build. The Minister said he felt obliged to have regard to the fact that the company bought the site on the clear understanding, after twice consulting the local planning authority in 1953 and 1956, that there would be no objection in principle to the site being used for the replacement of the existing garage.

Left and below: The pictures show the former British light-heavyweight wrestling champion, Frank Morgan, who wrestled under the name of Dai Sullivan. For a large part of his life, Frank lived in Warmsworth, at one time in the house of the present author, Peter Tuffrey. Francis (or Frank) Joseph Morgan was born in Tonypandy, South Wales, in 1921. He was a miner's son and at the age of five, moved with his family to Edlington, where his father obtained work at Yorkshire Main. On leaving school, Frank held several jobs before joining the Army at the outbreak of the Second World War. Around 1942, he became a physical training instructor and on leaving, he settled in Warmsworth, eventually establishing himself a reputation as a wrestler. He also became a stuntman in films. Perhaps the highlight of his wrestling career was tackling Lon Thez, the world heavyweight champion, in front of a capacity crowd at Leeds Town Hall. Frank died of a heart attack in 1983 at the relatively early age of 62. He had belonged to the heyday of wrestling, 1950-1970.

Scene at the Warmsworth rectory garden party, June 1955.

In October 1947, it was announced that a Warmsworth over sixties club was to be formed as a result of a meeting held at the White Lodge. Col. Warde-Aldam was to loan the old friends' meeting house in Quaker Lane, the interior of which can be seen here. In recent years, the house has been converted to a private dwelling.

Warmsworth Church of England school group. From left to right, back row: Raymond Fisher, Leslie Bennett, -?-, Paul Nelson, Irene Cook, Rita Bennett, Margaret Youdon, Janet Smith, Peter Reynolds, -?-, -?-, -?-. Third row includes Pamela Dungworth, Maureen Ayling, Brenda Emms. Second row includes Brian Gray, Alan Gray, Shiela Nelson. Front row -?-, -?-, Maureen Wallace, -?-, -?-, Angela Merrion, Jane Medley, Colin Bowser.

Warmsworth Church of England school group. Back row includes Michael Sadowski, Alan Gray, Carol Marsden, Edward Martin, Stephen Axon. Third row: Michael Mashin, Hilary Veale, Maureen Wallace, John Bigney, Pamela Dungworth, Brian Wood. Second row includes Ashley Norton, John Medley. Front row: Kenneth Mills, Christine Burgin, Marilyn Sharp, Graham Hill, Ian Terry.

Cecil Avenue, looking towards Sheffield Road. Similar to Wrightson Avenue, Cecil was built in stages, as can be seen by looking at an early picture of the thoroughfare on p. 94. Cecil was the maiden name of Lady Isabella Georgiana Katherine Battie-Wrightson, who married William Henry Thomas (later Battie-Wrightson), in August 1884. Lady Isabella was the eldest daughter of William Alleyne Cecil, third Marquis of Exeter of Burghley House, Stamford. The Battie-Wrightsons were formerly Lords of the Manor of Warmsworth and owned much of the land in and around the area.

Low Road West, looking towards the entrance to Warmsworth Hall. Quaker Lane is on the left. Much of the property along this thoroughfare, at the heart of what may be termed the old Warmsworth village, once belonged to the Warde-Aldam family.

The Cecil and Battie Wrightson Arms, on the right, was demolished for road widening during the 1960s, and a new pub was erected on a site set back. It also carries a more simple title: 'The Cecil'.

Opposite below: In December 1958 it was reported that the new multi-lane A1(M) motorway would mean the demolition of only one historical building: White House, which stood on a bad bend in the Sheffield to Doncaster road. The White House—a fine example of Georgian architecture, was built by the Aldam family. Mr and Mrs G.M. Frampton and Mrs Ethel Briggs were the White House's last tenants. Mrs Briggs said she had lived in the house for the last thirty-three years, but was told to leave. The other tenant, Mrs Frampton, said that while she and her husband had nowhere to go, they were not angry. 'Doncaster is very badly in need of a by-pass and you cannot stop progress.'

Right: Margaret Hempstock as the Warmsworth Gala Queen during the 1950s.

Below: The cast of the Christmas play at Warmsworth's Church of England school, Low Road West, December 1959. Those depicted include Simon Guyler, Michael Jones, John Squires, Charlie Mashin, Carol Webb, Tony Swift, Peter Tuffrey, John Wigley, Charles Day, William Bignall, Stephen Gater, Sandra Merrils, Elizabeth Gray, Elizabeth Highes, Susan Swaby, Jane Hough, Julie Burgin.

In January 1958, the *Doncaster Chronicle* reported that it was now possible for everyone to see just where the proposed A1(M) Doncaster by-pass would cut through the village. 'Drillers are at work alongside the Sheffield Road about 150 yards west of the Balby bus terminus, making site investigations. At that point the by-pass will go under the existing Sheffield Road ... Tenter Lane allotments will disappear; ... the roadmakers will have to construct a new bridge to span the River Don, the largest obstacle in the whole 16 miles of the by-pass. The drillers have bored to 70ft and found what they expected to find—marl clay and a considerable depth of magnesium limestone.' The above picture was taken on 8 August 1960.

Work on the A1(M) Doncaster by-pass, at Warmsworth, on 8 August 1960.

View along Church Lane, showing the Bothy, a summer house in the garden of the White House. The area was swept away during the construction of the A1(M).

The construction is under way of a bridge over the Doncaster-Sheffield railway at Warmsworth.

Plant machinery involved in the cutting out of a section of the A1(M) at Warmsworth.

Work on the bridge which spans the valley between Warmsworth and Sprotbrough during the construction of the A1(M).

Plant machinery involved in the cutting out of a section of the A1(M) at Warmsworth.

The new roundabout at Warmsworth takes shape.

Above: Widening the High Road, Warmsworth, during the early 1960s.

Below: The Parish Rooms, on the right, in August 1960. On 13 April 1961 the *Doncaster Chronicle* stated that due to the fact that the Old Parish Rooms were to be demolished, Warmsworth Youth Club has had to find a new home in the Mill Lane school.

Above and below: Saddler Fred Lowrey, whose premises were on High Road, Warmsworth. Fred Lowrey had not been a saddler all his life. His grandfather was a shoemaker, but after joining him for a couple of years after leaving school, Fred drifted from the leather trade until the Second World War. Then he became a saddler in the Royal Artillery, or to use the War Office description, 'Equipment Repairer'. After the War he decided to re-enter the leather trade and after a course at the Rural Industries school took over and converted the old smithy. At one time he had two assistants and one of these, Peter Kelly, is pictured below.

A trolleybus turning near the Blue Star garage during the late 1950s. The Blue Star company was born when ex-Etonian Maurice Deen, who started his working life at an oil refinery in Oklahoma, bought a piece of land in Hertfordshire. When work started on the Watford by-pass, Deen found himself with an ideal site for his first filling station. In his first ten years he added thirty more businesses. Some were developments of new sites, and others were businesses he bought up. The Blue Star garage was rebuilt during 1961.

Warmsworth Wasps at Mill Lane school, during the 1963/64 season. From left to right, back row: John Wigley, Charlie Mashin, Andrew Tasker, Peter Tuffrey, Trevor Turner, Malcolm Edees, Robert Edees. Front row: Robert Lane, Peter Curry, Tony Swift, Anthony Hewitt, Michael Edees.

Members of Warmsworth Cricket Club pose outside the pavilion. Those identified include Fred Curtis and Peter Nelson.

A lorry spills its load on the Warmsworth roundabout.

The children and staff of Warmsworth Low Road church of England infants' school saying goodbye to their old school on Friday 4 August 1978. The *Doncaster Evening Post* of 5 August 1978, reported: 'As the head teacher Mrs Audrey Green [with keys, top right] locked the door for the last time, yesterday there were a few tears, for it has been such a friendly, family type of school. "In many ways we are sorry to be leaving it. Lots of parents and grandparents of our children came here, and they all want to know if its going to be the same in the new school," said Mrs Green, who has been here since 1966. There are plans to convert the school, built in 1937, into a community centre after the children have moved into the new school which has been built nearby. The new school will cater for an extra age group, so instead of 81 four-to-seven year-olds, there will be about 110 four-to-eight year-olds. And Mrs Green's staff of three full-time teachers, [from left to right] Mrs Hodgkinson, Mrs G. Pouberth, and Mrs M. Broadbent, will be augmented by an additional teacher.' In recent times, however, the new school has closed.